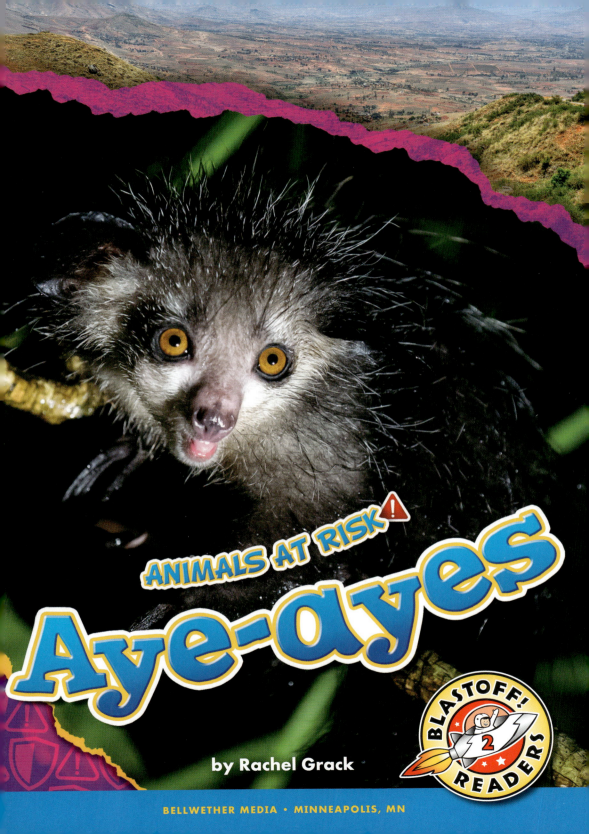

ANIMALS AT RISK

Aye-ayes

by Rachel Grack

BLASTOFF! READERS

BELLWETHER MEDIA • MINNEAPOLIS, MN

Blastoff! Readers are carefully developed by literacy experts to build reading stamina and move students toward fluency by combining standards-based content with developmentally appropriate text.

LEVELS

Level 1 provides the most support through repetition of high-frequency words, light text, predictable sentence patterns, and strong visual support.

Level 2 offers early readers a bit more challenge through varied sentences, increased text load, and text-supportive special features.

Level 3 advances early-fluent readers toward fluency through increased text load, less reliance on photos, advancing concepts, longer sentences, and more complex special features.

★ **Blastoff! Universe**

Reading Level

Grade K

Grades 1–3

Grade 4

This edition first published in 2025 by Bellwether Media, Inc.

No part of this publication may be reproduced in whole or in part without written permission of the publisher. For information regarding permission, write to Bellwether Media, Inc., Attention: Permissions Department, 6012 Blue Circle Drive, Minnetonka, MN 55343.

Library of Congress Cataloging-in-Publication Data

LC record for Aye-ayes available at: https://lccn.loc.gov/2024009425

Text copyright © 2025 by Bellwether Media, Inc. BLASTOFF! READERS and associated logos are trademarks and/or registered trademarks of Bellwether Media, Inc. Bellwether Media is a division of Chrysalis Education Group.

Editor: Kieran Downs   Designer: Brittany McIntosh

Printed in the United States of America, North Mankato, MN.

Table of Contents

Strange Climbers   4
In Danger!   8
Save the Aye-ayes!   12
Glossary   22
To Learn More   23
Index   24

Strange Climbers

Aye-ayes are **nocturnal** lemurs. They are strange-looking **primates**.

They have big ears and round eyes. Their long, bony fingers help them dig **insects** out of trees.

Aye-ayes live in forests in Madagascar. They climb high in trees.

Aye-ayes once had greater numbers. But they are now **endangered**. People have caused their biggest troubles.

Aye-aye Range

range =

In Danger!

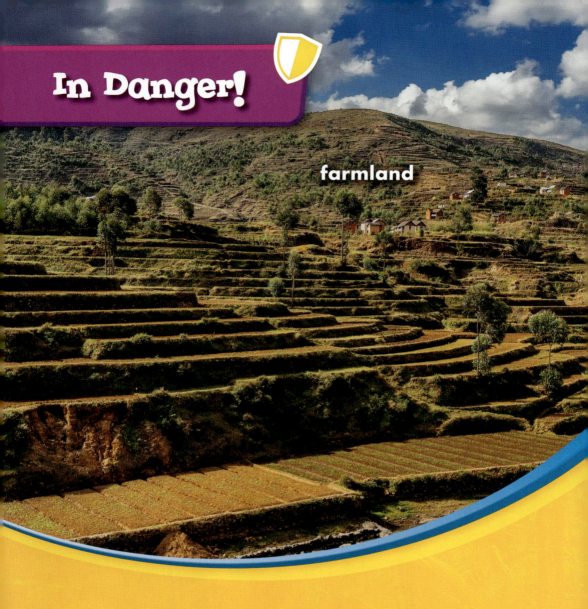

farmland

Aye-aye **habitats** keep getting smaller. People cut down trees for **timber**. They clear land for farms.

Climate change
also destroys aye-ayes' forest homes.

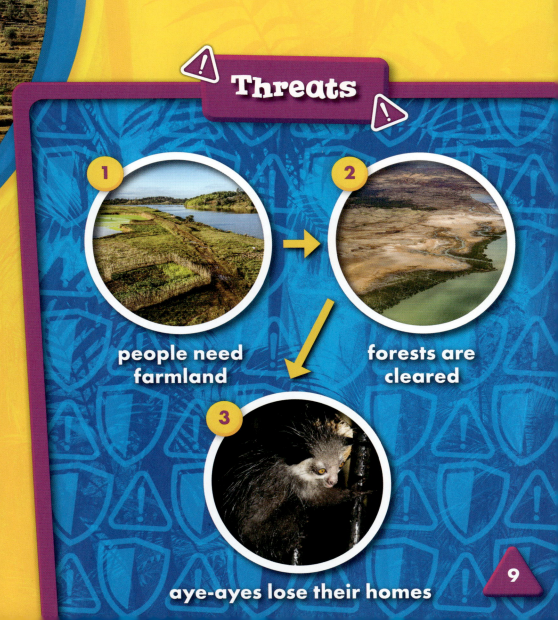

Threats

1. people need farmland
2. forests are cleared
3. aye-ayes lose their homes

Some **cultures** believe aye-ayes bring bad luck. People are quick to harm them.

Farmers also get rid of aye-ayes to **protect** their crops.

Aye-aye Stats

| Least Concern | Near Threatened | Vulnerable | Endangered | Critically Endangered | Extinct in the Wild | Extinct |

conservation status: endangered

life span: up to 20 years

Save the Aye-ayes!

Aye-ayes help their habitats.
They eat fruit and spread seeds.
This helps plants grow.

Some beetles harm trees. Aye-ayes eat beetle **larvae**. Forests stay healthy.

The World with Aye-ayes

1  2

more aye-ayes

seeds spread

3

more trees and plants grow

13

Madagascar's government set up **reserves** for aye-ayes. People cannot clear this land.

reserve

Wildlife workers study aye-ayes to learn new ways to help them.

Farmers can replant **native** trees around their crops. The trees **fertilize** the soil.

Crops grow better and forests grow bigger. Aye-ayes may one day have larger habitats.

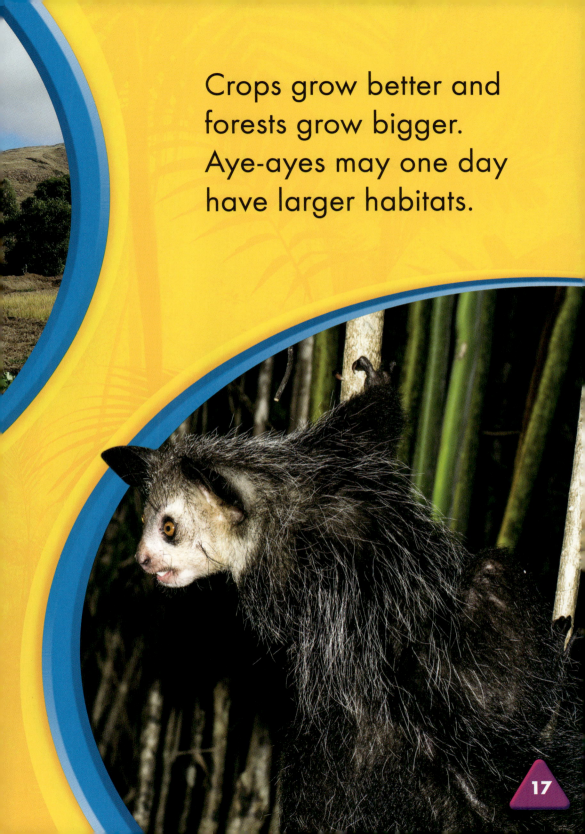

Children of Madagascar learn about aye-ayes in school. They take a special class.

It teaches them how to care for nature and wildlife.

There are many ways to help aye-ayes. **Donations** help wildlife workers care for aye-ayes. Using less **energy** slows climate change.

Together, everyone can save these nighttime climbers!

Glossary

climate change—a human-caused change in Earth's weather due to warming temperatures

cultures—groups of people with the same customs and beliefs

donations—gifts for a certain cause; most donations are money.

endangered—in danger of dying out

energy—the power to make things work

fertilize—to make soil better for growing plants

habitats—the places where animals live

insects—small animals with six legs and bodies divided into three parts

larvae—young insects that break out of eggs and look like small worms

native—originally from a certain place

nocturnal—active at night

primates—animals that use their hands to grasp food and other objects

protect—to keep safe

reserves—lands set aside for wildlife

timber—wood that is used for building

To Learn More

AT THE LIBRARY

Bassier, Emma. *Aye-ayes*. North Mankato, Minn.: Pop!, 2020.

Terp, Gail. *Aye-ayes*. Mankato, Minn.: Black Rabbit Books, 2023.

Watt, E. Melanie. *Aye-ayes*. New York, N.Y.: Lightbox Learning, 2023.

ON THE WEB

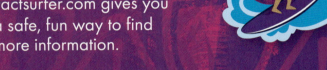

Factsurfer.com gives you a safe, fun way to find more information.

1. Go to www.factsurfer.com.

2. Enter "aye-ayes" into the search box and click 🔍.

3. Select your book cover to see a list of related content.

Index

beetles, 13
children, 18
class, 18
climate change, 9, 20
crops, 10, 16, 17
cultures, 10
donations, 20
ears, 5
endangered, 7
energy, 20
eyes, 5
farmers, 10, 16
farms, 8
fingers, 5
forests, 6, 9, 13, 17
fruit, 12
government, 14
habitats, 8, 12, 17
insects, 5
land, 8, 14
larvae, 13
lemurs, 4
Madagascar, 6, 14, 18

numbers, 7
people, 7, 8, 10, 14
plants, 12
primates, 4
range, 6, 7
reserves, 14
seeds, 12
soil, 16
stats, 11
threats, 9
timber, 8
trees, 5, 6, 8, 13, 16
ways to help, 20
wildlife workers, 15, 20
world with, 13

The images in this book are reproduced through the courtesy of: Eugen Haag, front cover, pp. 9 (bottom), 10-11, 13 (left), 20-21; Artush, front cover (tear), pp. 3, 9 (right), 23; Danita Delimont/ Alamy, p. 4; Aflo, p. 5; Nature Picture Library/ Alamy, p. 6; Veranika848, p. 8; Pierre-Yves Babelon, p. 9 (left); Nick Garbutt, p. 10; Ariadne Van Zandbergen/ Alamy, pp. 12, 18; Yuphayao Pooh's 13 (right); Damian Ryszawy, 13 (bottom); Hugh Lansdown, p. 14; Gabbro/ Alamy, p. 15; Arwen Matthijssen, p. 16; Konstantin Kalishko/ Alamy, p. 17; javarman, p. 19; Adrian Sherratt/ Alamy, p. 20.